MW01677779

contents

prologue

Who would think that a middle-aged African-American woman, weary from her day's work, would start the **AMERICAN CIVIL RIGHTS MOVEMENT**?

Or that a struggling, tongue-tied Indian lawyer would set in motion the Indian Independence Movement? And that, during World War II, a little-known German Lutheran pastor would give a radio address attacking the Nazi regime and then oppose it publicly until he was finally arrested, sent to a concentration camp and hanged.

author purpose

Why do you think the author wrote this prologue?

Heroes such as Martin Luther King and Dietrich Bonhoeffer didn't choose where they were born, or what circumstances they were born into. What they did choose were their actions.

THEY EACH MADE A PROFOUND DIFFERENCE

because they refused to accept the unacceptable; they chose to act.

How do we define heroes? Consider this following definition: a hero is an ordinary person, thrust into extraordinary circumstances, who chooses to act.

predict

How do you think the author will portray the person in this biography?

in the beginning

Velma B Johnston did not arrive on Earth with the halo of a hero. But, like other heroes, she chose not to accept the unacceptable. She chose to act. This is her story – the story of a woman who refused to accept the cruel and senseless destruction of wild horse herds in her homeland.

propaganda

Do you think the author is trying to influence your opinion of Wild Horse Annie? If so, explain how.

THIS IS THE STORY OF WILD HORSE ANNIE...

Velma Johnston, the eldest of four children, was born on March 5, 1912, in Reno, Nevada, to ranchers Joseph Bronn and Gertrude Clay. Velma often felt that she had wild horse blood in her veins thanks to her father.

Family stories told how, when her father's pioneering family came to California from Nevada in a covered wagon, they were plagued by bad weather and dwindling food rations.

JOSEPH'S MOTHER BECAME UNABLE TO FEED HER NEWBORN SON,

but a wild range mare and her foal were travelling alongside the wagon and the mare's milk was used to save Joseph's life.

Like her father, Velma met with peril when, at the age of 11, she contracted polio (a disease that often causes paralysis and muscle wasting).

clarify
- profound
- empathy
- compassion
- all-consuming

SHE SPENT MONTHS IN HOSPITAL,

confined in a body cast that left her disfigured for life.

This devastating experience created in her a profound empathy and compassion for the suffering of other creatures.

At school, teased and taunted for her deformity, she threw herself into her schoolwork to escape. She loved writing poetry and drawing and she found comfort in looking after the animals on her parents' ranch.

As a young adult, Velma fell in love. She married Charlie Johnston, a part Delaware Indian from West Virginia, and they took over a ranch in Wadsworth, Nevada, called the Double Lazy Heart.

Unable to have children of their own, Velma and Charlie opened the ranch to school children, including many who had been in trouble in the city. They ran horses on the ranch to provide opportunities for riding. But Velma's life was to be changed by an all-consuming passion to put things right.

bias
Do you think the text demonstrates an author bias? Why/why not?

VELMA OFTEN FELT THAT SHE HAD WILD HORSE BLOOD IN HER VEINS THANKS TO HER FATHER

taking up the fight

The passion to fight for the wild horses took over Velma's life on a clear, beautiful morning as she drove to work in Nevada. A truck hauling livestock suddenly cut in front of her car.

THROUGH THE SLATS, SHE SAW HORSES – DESTINED TO BE PROCESSED INTO CHICKEN FEED – packed in so tightly they couldn't move. Dark liquid dripped from the truck's trailer. Straining to see what the liquid was, she was shocked to discover it was blood coming from a foal…a foal no more than a few months old that lay floundering on the floor, trapped between two large horses on either side.

visual features

What effect does the design and illustration/photo have on you? Why?

HORSES FELL OF

SHE CHOSE TO ACT

clarify
discreetly
inflicted
carnage
expose

When the truck pulled into a slaughterhouse, Velma discreetly pulled in after it and parked her car in a place hidden from the plant's workers. She watched as a worker opened the trailer gate into a holding pen.

HORSES FELL OFF THE SIDES OF THE RAMP, TOPPLING OVER EACH OTHER,

scrambling to get to their feet. Most of them were severely injured. Parts of their hides had been stripped from their sides when they were roped and dragged up the trailer ramp. Many of them were peppered with red dots – the marks of gunshot wounds inflicted by mustang hunters.

As the miserable occupants straggled out, one stayed behind – the small foal had been trampled to death on the trailer floor.

Witnessing this slaughterhouse carnage changed the path of Velma's life. She chose to act and expose the suffering of these wild horses to the public eye. The year was 1950.

emotive appeal
How has the author used language to influence the reader's response?

THE
IDES OF THE RAMP

opinion

Why do you think Wild Horse Annie used photographic documentation to expose the round-up issues to the public?

During her childhood, Velma had listened to stories about wild horse "round-ups" but, though she found the accounts disturbing, she did nothing.

> She later wrote, *"Although I had heard that airplanes were being used to capture mustangs, like so many of us do when something doesn't touch our lives directly, I pretended it didn't concern me. But, one morning in the year 1950, my apathetic attitude was jarred into acute awareness. What had now touched my life was to reach into the lives of many others as time went on."*

Haunted by the image of the trampled foal, Velma went to see a round-up for herself. Armed with a camera, she hunched on top of her car and, much like a private investigator, secretly documented the horrific scene before her. The danger she put herself in as a consequence of her actions is clear in a *Time* magazine article dated July 27, 1959. The article describes how Charlie sat in the car with a .38 calibre revolver on his lap as Velma snapped photographs on the roof.

clarify

apathetic
acute

"Wild Horse Annie" Bill

The wild horses and burros of the romantic Old West are fast disappearing. Until 15 years ago they still galloped over the western hills and grasslands in great herds, but since World War II an estimated 100,000 have been captured and cut up for dog food. Today, the Department of Interior estimates that no more than 20,000 wild horses still graze on the lone prairies. Last week the wild horses had their day in Congress.

Their frail, unlikely-looking champion, Mrs. Velma B Johnston, 47, is a Reno secretary. Ten years ago she was shocked to see a truckload of frightened, bleeding wild horses on their way to the slaughterhouse. She investigated the methods of the round-up and was even more deeply disturbed. She then launched a campaign that has won her the nickname "Wild Horse Annie".

For two hours last week, Wild Horse Annie told her story to 16 interested members of a House judiciary subcommittee. The mustangs are flushed from their hilly retreats by low-flying airplanes, whose pilots pursue the animals across the prairies until they are near exhaustion. Then trucks take up the chase. Finally, the horses are lassoed with ropes weighted with truck tyres or other heavy objects. The horses drag the weights around until they drop. Then they are hobbled and hauled into the truck. Wild Horse Annie documented all this with photographs that she took from the top of her car, while her husband sat below, a .38 revolver in his lap.

personal response

...like so many of us do when something doesn't touch our lives directly, I pretended it didn't concern me.

How can you relate to this situation? Give an example from personal experience.

ATTITUDE

AWARENESS

Velma's account of the round-up presented the public with a graphically chilling window into the extreme, gratuitous brutality of the capture:

The mustangs are driven, at breakneck speed, by planes, from their meagre refuge in the rough and barren rim rock into flatlands or dry lake beds. There the chase is taken up by hunters standing on fast-moving pickup trucks, and the exhausted mustangs, after a run of 15 to 20 miles speeded by swooping planes, many of them carrying bullet wounds inflicted to make them run faster, are easy victims for ropers. Once the running horse is roped, a heavy truck tyre tied to the other end of the rope is thrown out of the truck.

THE FRANTIC HORSE WITH HIS SIDES HEAVING AND BLOOD RUNNING FROM HIS NOSTRILS

soon falls exhausted, and his feet are quickly trussed. Another line is then attached to his hind legs and he is pulled up a plank ramp into the bed of the truck. The ropes are removed and the animal is prodded to his feet. Frequently the hide is stripped from his side during the drag up the board ramp… Others, too badly hurt to load, are left to die from the injuries received in the long pursuit by plane and truck. Young colts are frequently abandoned and starve to death…

clarify

graphically chilling window
gratuitous brutality
trussed

language and visual features

What effect does the choice of language, illustration and design on this spread have on you?
Has it influenced your response to the issue? Why/why not?

Velma discovered that often the horses driven to exhaustion would be left behind by the mustang hunters to be gathered later, their nostrils wired shut so they could barely breathe.

The "lucky" ones died on the spot; others were shot, wounded and left to die. Surviving horses were crushed into trains or trucks for transportation – without food or water – to the rendering plants. Many were packed so tightly that, when they died, they remained standing. There was no room for them to fall.

inference

What can you infer about the types of people the mustang hunters were?

THERE WAS NO ROOM FOR THEM TO FALL

gathering the facts

Velma knew as she gathered information that the unfettered slaughter decimated the mustang herds.

At the turn of the 20th century, an estimated **TWO MILLION WILD HORSES THUNDERED OVER THE DESERTS** and grasslands of North America. Valued for transportation and agriculture, the horse was the backbone of native and settler life. But by the 1920s, with automobiles in use and tractors introduced to agriculture, the dependence on the horse was broken. Many unwanted horses were released into the wild, causing the mustang population to burgeon. Ranchers viewed the wild herds as nuisances that competed with their cattle for grazing land.

establishing the facts

What resources could Wild Horse Annie have used to establish the facts on the exploitation of wild horses? How would you go about this research today?

COMPETE

clarify

- unfettered
- decimated
- burgeon
- exploitation
- outlaws

For the next 30 years, federally unregulated exploitation and slaughter of the wild horse for meat ravaged the herds. The processing of horsemeat into food for animals and humans reached its height in the 1930s, resulting in the production of almost 14 million kilograms. An article in *Time* magazine, February 20, 1939, reported:

ONE COMPANY ALONE KILLED 300,000 HORSES.

> *In five years (1925-1930) the Schlessers [Schlesser Bros, the world's biggest packers of horsemeat at that time] slaughtered some 300,000 head of outlaws, salted their meat in 51-gallon barrels and shipped them overseas…hooves, ears, tails were sold for glue and oil; ground bones and scraps for chicken feed; hides for baseballs and shoes; blood for fertiliser, casings for German sausage…*

opinion

What is your opinion about eating horses and using their by-products? Why do you think this?

ANCHERS VIEWED THE WILD ERDS AS NUISANCES THAT VITH THEIR CATTLE FOR GRAZING LAND

Velma Johnston diligently gathered evidence for her campaign against the wholesale slaughter, knowing that, in order to have any influence, **SHE WOULD NEED HARD FACTS.**

Her father had wisely told her that her campaign could be easily disregarded by her opponents as the ranting of an "overly emotional female" if she wasn't careful. As she said, *"You see, because I am a woman, I cannot afford to indulge in anything bordering on the sentimental, lest I be judged over-emotional... What personal feelings I have are something different."*

Velma was well aware that women in the 1950s had very confined roles and stepping into a political arena against the meat industry – run by powerful ranchers and mustang hunters – made the odds against her high, as were the risks.

Inference

What can you infer about the way women were viewed by society in the 1950s?

Throughout Velma's campaign, her life was often in jeopardy – one rancher even said that he would like to see her made into a case of dog food. Particularly in the early stages of her battle, the situation was so precarious that **VELMA ANSWERED HER DOOR HOLDING A GUN BEHIND HER BACK!**

clarify
diligently
confined
precarious

WOMEN IN THE 1950s HAD VERY CONFINED ROLES

beyond the text

How would you set up a campaign to save wild horses today? How would it differ from a campaign in the 1950s and 60s?

changing
the rules

clarify
- vehement
- detractors
- unwittingly
- legislative

During a debate in the Nevada State Legislature, one of Velma's most vehement detractors jeeringly called her "Wild Horse Annie" in an attempt to embarrass and discredit her.

THERE WOULD BE MANY SUCH ATTACKS TO COME BUT VELMA ASKED HER FRIENDS TO CALL HER ANNIE, SO THEY WOULD NEVER FORGET WHAT THEY WERE UP AGAINST.

In fact, her opponent had unwittingly branded Velma's cause by creating a nickname so catchy it focused attention on the fight for legislative change more effectively than a multi-million-dollar advertising campaign!

language feature

Irony – a contradiction between the expected outcome of a situation and the actual results. Find the example of irony on this page.

Velma added another weapon to her fight: school children. Visiting schools and talking to the children about the mustang round-ups, she aroused such empathy and pity for the horses that children wrote letters by the thousands. Congress was deluged with letters about the mustang round-ups.

One child's letter read:

Dear Wild Horse Annie, Today I read your article about the wild horses. When I saw those pictures I started crying. How can people be so cruel? Why can't we let the wild ones go their own way? Why can't we let them roam free in body and in spirit? Please, Annie, I'm only 11 but I want to help.

opinion

Do you think Velma should have used school children in her campaign? Why/why not?

beyond the text

How would you respond to a visit to your classroom by Wild Horse Annie? Would you be caught up in the cause? How would you establish whether the cause was worthy?

clarify

unswerving sense of justice

Velma drew support from anyone who could help: school children, sympathetic ranchers, housewives, environmentalists, businessmen and politicians. The unswerving sense of justice in her public speeches touched her audiences. In her campaign to woo the American people, she referred frequently to the idea that,

"MUSTANGS REPRESENT THE KIND OF FREEDOM THIS COUNTRY WAS FOUNDED ON".

Letters from all around the world flowed in and Velma responded to each and every one with information and specific instructions on how they could help.

emotive appeal

"MUSTANGS REPRESENT THE KIND OF FREEDOM THIS COUNTRY WAS FOUNDED ON."

What kind of emotive response do you think Velma was trying to evoke from her audience with this statement?

SHE SPOKE WITH AN UNSWERVING SENSE OF JUSTICE

She wrote of her support: "*Offers to help have come from every state, and people in all walks of life have joined the fight – ministers, housewives, students, teachers, sportsmen, the nuns in a convent in the East, a blind man who read the story in Braille, men in the armed forces in faraway places, lawyers, doctors and people of all ages; the youngest a potential Miss America of six, and the eldest a one-time cowpoke in his 80s, who could well remember the wild ones he'd 'broke and rode'.*"

inference

What can you infer about how Velma managed to get support from people all over the world?

Velma's campaign began to effect change. In 1955 the Nevada State Legislature signed a bill banning aircraft and land vehicles from round-ups on state land. But, since that bill did nothing to protect horses on federal land, Velma pressed on. Finally, in 1959, a federal law known as the Wild Horse Annie Act was enacted, prohibiting the use of motorised vehicles in round-ups on public land and prohibiting the poisoning of water holes in order to kill or capture mustangs.

Wild Horse Annie Act –
Public Law 86-234

Use of aircraft or motor vehicles to hunt certain wild horses or burros; pollution of watering holes.

(a) Whoever uses an aircraft or a motor vehicle to hunt, for the purpose of capturing or killing, any wild unbranded horse, mare, colt, or burro running at large on any of the public land or ranges shall be fined under this title, or imprisoned for not more than six months, or both.

(b) Whoever pollutes or causes the pollution of any watering hole on any of the public land or ranges for the purpose of trapping, killing, wounding, or maiming any of the animals referred to in subsection (a) of this section shall be fined under this title, or imprisoned for not more than six months, or both.

(c) As used in subsection (a) of this section:

(1) The term "aircraft" means any contrivance used for flight in the air; and

(2) The term "motor vehicle" includes an automobile, automobile truck, automobile wagon, motorcycle, or any other self-propelled vehicle designed for running on land.

question

How do you think the Wild Horse Annie Act was enforced in the 1960s?

reading between the lines

Do you think the author has been dispassionate in writing about her subject? Why/why not? What evidence do you have?

VELMA'S CAMPAIGN BEGAN TO EFFECT CHANGE

rewards and setbacks

Velma's campaign was an incredible accomplishment and, after the legislation was passed, **THE MASSACHUSETTS SOCIETY FOR THE PREVENTION OF CRUELTY TO ANIMALS** presented her with the Humanitarian of the Year Award.

In her acceptance speech, she said: *"Have you ever wondered how it feels to touch a star? I can pretty well tell you about it now. The feeling is a combination of many things…of exhilaration at the successful accomplishment of a difficult job…*

OF UNSHAKEABLE FAITH IN THE ABILITY OF THE INDIVIDUAL TO SUCCEED IN HIS ENDEAVOURS EVENTUALLY…

of a sublime belief in the great capacity of the human mind and heart for goodness and compassion…profound joy, because children, little and big, in their many different ways, responded to the dire plight of their animal friends – their letters of thanks, misspellings and all, are worthy of a special place in a treasure chest of important things…"

language features

What effect does Velma's use of language have on you? Has it influenced your opinion of her? Why/why not?

clarify

sublime belief
flagrant violations

Soon after the legislation was enacted, Charlie became terminally ill and died just 11 months later. The marriage had lasted for 27 years and Charlie had been the great love of Velma's life. Without Charlie at her side, she fought on alone.

IN THE MID 1960s IT BECAME CLEAR THAT THE FIGHT TO PROTECT THE WILD HORSE WAS NOT OVER.

Mustang populations continued to dwindle, with flagrant violations of the law. Subsequent failures to convict the offenders were well documented.

Friends and supporters helped Velma to regroup and continue the fight. She wrote of her decision: *"When Charlie and I were a team, no hill was too high…no challenge too great… I suppose I am not using good judgement in taking on so tough a fight…for the second time in my life, with limited time, health, finances and a decade added to my age, but, having spent the great part of the last 18 years witnessing the unspeakably cruel destiny of the wild ones, it would not be characteristic of me to turn my back on them until the last victorious plateau is reached…"*

inference

What can you infer about the way Velma sees herself from this quotation?

Velma continued to educate and galvanise the public to pressure the government for the implementation of permanent protection. Finally, in 1971, the Wild Free-Roaming Horse and Burro Act (P.L. 92-195) was passed unanimously and signed into law.

clarify

- galvanise
- implementation
- testimonies
- instrumental
- instigated

It stated that the mustangs should be free from capture, branding, harassment or death. The Bureau of Land Management was assigned to enforce this law. Fines of up to $2000 and a jail sentence gave the law enforcers the teeth to deal with those who violated the Act.

REMAINING VIGILANT VELMA AND HER DEVOTED TEAM KEPT UP SURVEILLANCE ON THE WILD HORSE HERDS TO ENSURE THEIR CONTINUED PROTECTION

Files of field notes (many in Velma's own handwriting), including maps and photographs, as well as eyewitness testimonies, are kept by organisations that Velma helped establish, such as the International Society for the Protection of Mustangs and Burros (ISPMB) and Wild Horses Organised Assistance (WHOA).

question generate

What further questions do you have about Wild Horse Annie?

GALLOP ACROSS THE PLAINS WITH MANES AND TAILS FLYING IN THE WIND NOSTRILS FLARED AN EYES REFLECTING THEIR LOVE OF FREEDOM

Velma was also instrumental in establishing wild horse refuges – the largest was established in 1966, at the Nellis Air Force Base in southern Nevada. Other refuges instigated by Velma include Pryor Mountain refuge, on the Montana/Wyoming border, and Little Bookcliffs, near Palisade, Colorado, where a monument to Velma B "Wild Horse Annie" Johnston stands.

opinion

How well has the author portrayed Velma Johnston? Support your answer with a character web to help summarise what you now know/ don't know.

Velma died in 1977 but her legacy to the wild horses of the United States lives on. Today the herds are a part of the national heritage and they continue to gallop across the plains with manes and tails flying in the wind, nostrils flared and eyes reflecting their love of freedom.

personal response

If you were reviewing this biography, what would you say? In your view, how does the author rate as a biographer?

epilogue

THE BATTLE FOR THE WILD HORSE CONTINUES.

In 2004, a one-page rider buried in a 3300-page bill passed by Congress gutted the 1971 law intended to protect the mustangs. Rider number 142 removes all protections for horses and burros over the age of 10, or that have failed to be adopted three times.

The rider claims that the horses are "overgrazing" the land and the mustangs and burros can now be sold *"without limitation, including through auction to the highest bidder, at local saleyards or other convenient livestock-selling facilities"*.

Wild horse advocates argue that the Wild Free-Roaming Horse and Burro Act, brought into law by massive letter-writing campaigns, worldwide concern and democratic procedure, has been circumvented, adapted and gutted, leaving the "wild ones" as vulnerable now as they were in Velma's day. They argue that, since there are millions of livestock grazing public land (for a nominal fee) and only meagre numbers of horses, it is not the horses that are overgrazing.

clarify

- rider
- democratic procedure
- circumvented
- monopolistic
- travesty

Velma wrote: *"The commercial exploitation of mustangs is one of the blackest instances in the history of our treatment of animals, and that it has been encouraged and allowed to continue is a reflection upon the lethargic people and bureau that have permitted its continuation…*
The public is becoming fed up with the monopolistic, possessive attitude of the users of the public lands."

Her words are as true today as they were when she wrote them.

author purpose

Why do you think the author wrote an epilogue? What messages did she want to convey?

Karen Sussman, president of the International Society for the Protection of Mustangs and Burros, wrote:

> *"We have fewer wild horses and burros now than we did in 1971, when the law was passed, stating that 'wild horses and burros were fast disappearing from the American scene'. We have about 23,000 wild horses and only about 4000 wild burros. It is a travesty."*

The story of Velma's fight to save the mustang isn't a fairytale – the ending is still unfolding, with new generations picking up where the old left off. But the fact that we still have wild horses to protect and defend is due to the efforts of this extraordinary ordinary woman who simply *chose to act.*

As Dr Martin Luther King Jr said, *"Not everyone can be famous, but everyone can be great, because greatness is determined by service."*

IT IS THE DECISION TO ACT THAT DEFINES US – THE ANSWER TO THE QUESTION... WHY?

THE COMMERCIAL EXPLOITATION OF MUSTANGS IS ONE OF THE BLACKEST INSTANCES IN THE HISTORY OF OUR TREATMENT OF ANIMALS

beyond the text

How would you describe a hero? What helped you make your definition? Is Velma Johnston a hero in your eyes? Why/why not?

think about the text

MAKING CONNECTIONS

What connections can you make to the life of Velma Johnston and her cause?

TEXT TO SELF

- facing ridicule
- persevering against the odds
- facing setbacks
- being afraid of repercussions
- motivating people into action
- not accepting the unacceptable
- fighting for a cause

TEXT TO TEXT

Discuss what connections you can make between this text and other media you have read or seen.

TEXT TO WORLD

Discuss other situations or issues in the world that connect to elements in this text.

planning a biography

1 CHOOSE AN INTERESTING PERSON who you think will captivate the interest of the reader. Write some questions that will help you to define, explore and document what makes his/her life extraordinary.

- **what** sort of family/society did he/she come from?
- **what** was his/her childhood like?
- **what** education did he/she have?
- **what** events shaped or changed his/her life?
- **what** were his/her achievements?
- **what** effect did he/she have on the world/other people?
- **did** he/she overcome obstacles, take risks, experience luck?
- **how** significant was his/her contribution to society?

2 DO THE RESEARCH to provide answers to your questions and evidence for your conclusions.

- **interview** the person or his/her connections.
- **search** for information from the library and/or the Internet and check its authenticity by cross-referencing.
- **search** for documentation that records details of his/her life, eg, birth/death certificates, marriage certificates, newspaper/magazine reports…

3 LOOK AT YOUR INFORMATION and note key points.

Make a plan using your key points in a logical sequence. Incorporate appropriate visuals in your plan.

PROLOGUE

- Introducing idea of power of one person in fighting wrong

KEY POINTS IN SEQUENCE

- Velma's early family life
- Events that sparked the taking up of her cause – photos/visuals, media reports, letters

"Wild Horse Annie" Bill

- Sequence of actions taken
- How other people saw her actions
- Changing the rules – letters from public, media reports summarising her success
- The ongoing effects of Velma's work

EPILOGUE

- Conclusionary statement

4 USE YOUR PLAN TO WRITE THE BIOGRAPHY

writing a biography

have you. . .

- Cross-referenced your information?
- Included significant information and excluded unnecessary information?
- Provided a sequence of events that makes sense and is easy to follow?
- Provided an authentic and accurate portrayal of your subject?
- Checked for omissions?
- Included relevant visuals, such as documents, photographs and media reports, as supporting evidence?
- Included relevant quotes, anecdotes or comments from other people?

. . .don't forget to revisit your writing.

do you need to change, add or delete anything to improve your biography?

mainsails 4

BIOGRAPHY / MEMOIR

ISBN 978-1-86970-603-6

Pearson Heinemann